Celebrations in My World

Remembrance Day

Crabtree Publishing Company
www.crabtreebooks.com

Molly
Aloian

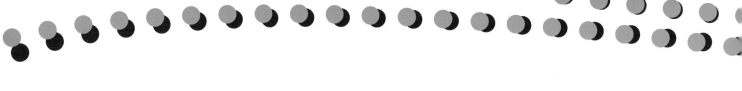

Crabtree Publishing Company
www.crabtreebooks.com

Author: Molly Aloian
Coordinating editor: Chester Fisher
Series editor: Susan LaBella
Editor: Adrianna Morganelli
Proofreader: Reagan Miller
Editorial director: Kathy Middleton
Production coordinator: Katherine Berti
Prepress technician: Katherine Berti
Project manager: Kumar Kunal (Q2AMEDIA)
Art direction: Rahul Dhiman (Q2AMEDIA)
Cover design: Cheena Yadav (Q2AMEDIA)
Design: Ritu Chopra, Cheena Yadav (Q2AMEDIA)
Photo research: Ekta Sharma (Q2AMEDIA)

Photographs:
123RF: Keith Levit: p. 17
Alamy: Icpix Can: p. 14; David Chapman: p. 18; Seapix: p. 12
AP Photo: Peter Dejong: p. 15; Clifford Skarstedt: p. 30
Corbis: Michael Macor/San Francisco Chronicle: p. 22
CP Photo: Halifax Chronicle Herald/Tim Krochak: cover, p. 21
Dreamstime: p. 25; Daniel Dupuis: p. 11; V J Matthew: p. 6
First Light: Toronto Star: p. 29
Fotolia: p. 13
Istockphoto: Adrian Beesley: p. 20
Photolibrary: Mark Cator: p. 26; Visions LLC: p. 27
Photostogo: p. 16
Reuters: Marko Djurica: p. 5; Daniel More: p. 7; Finbarr O'Reilly: p. 31;
    Pascal Rossignol: p. 9; Chris Wattie: p. 1, 4; Jim Young: p. 19
Shutterstock: p. 8; M. Dykstra: p. 23; Andrew Horwitz: folio image,
    p. 28; Sergey Kamshylin: p. 28; Roger de Montfort: p. 10;
    Tatyana Morozova: p. 28; Oleg Zabielin: p. 28
Reproduced with the permission of Veterans Affairs Canada, 2009: p. 24

Library and Archives Canada Cataloguing in Publication

Aloian, Molly
    Remembrance Day / Molly Aloian.

(Celebrations in my world)
Includes index.
ISBN 978-0-7787-4765-9 (bound).--ISBN 978-0-7787-4783-3 (pbk.)

    1. Remembrance Day (Canada)--Juvenile literature.
I. Title. II. Series: Celebrations in my world

D680.C2A46 2009   j394.264   C2009-905259-8

Library of Congress Cataloging-in-Publication Data

Aloian, Molly.
  Remembrance Day / Molly Aloian.
     p. cm. -- (Celebrations in my world)
  Includes index.
  ISBN 978-0-7787-4783-3 (pbk. : alk. paper) -- ISBN 978-0-7787-4765-9
(reinforced library binding : alk. paper)
  1. Remembrance Day (Canada)--Juvenile literature. I. Title. II. Series.

  D680.C2A45 2010
  394.264--dc22
                                                                2009034880

Crabtree Publishing Company

Printed in China/122009/CT20090915

www.crabtreebooks.com   1-800-387-7650

Published in Canada
Crabtree Publishing
616 Welland Ave.
St. Catharines, ON
L2M 5V6

Published in the United States
Crabtree Publishing
350 Fifth Ave.
59th floor
New York, NY 10118

Published in the United Kingdom
Crabtree Publishing
Maritime House
Basin Road North, Hove
BN41 1WR

Published in Australia
Crabtree Publishing
386 Mt. Alexander Rd.
Ascot Vale (Melbourne)
VIC 3032

Contents

What is Remembrance Day?

• This war memorial is in France.

Remembrance Day is a special day in Canada and in many other countries around the world. It takes place on November 11 each year. On this day, people remember and **honor** the men and women who serve their country during times of war and other **conflicts**.

DID YOU KNOW?

The first Remembrance Day was held on November 11, 1919, throughout the **Commonwealth**. *It was called Armistice Day.*

This picture shows a World War I cemetery.

On Remembrance Day, people honor men and women who fought and continue to fight in wars. Honoring these people shows appreciation for their actions. They fought and some lost their lives so that other people could live in peace.

Why Remember?

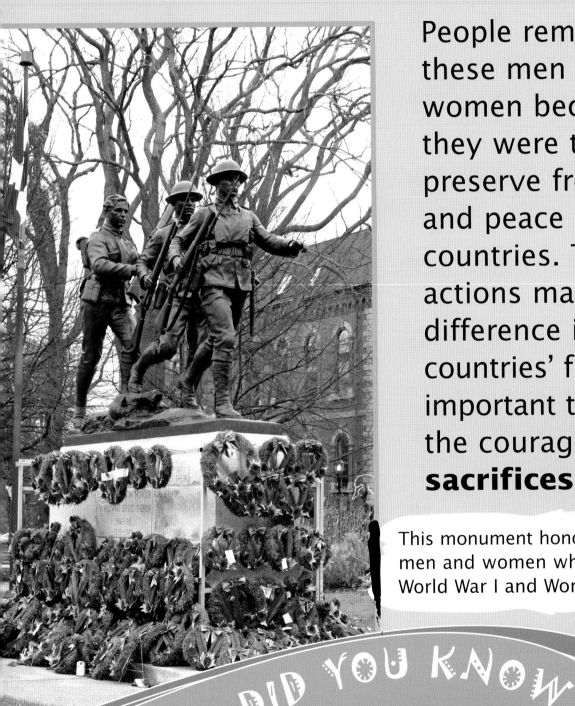

People remember these men and women because they were trying to preserve freedom and peace in their countries. Their actions made a difference in their countries' future. It is important to recognize the courage and **sacrifices** of others.

This monument honors the Canadian men and women who fought in World War I and World War II.

DID YOU KNOW?

More than 1.5 million Canadians have served during times of war.

On Remembrance Day, people recognize the hardships others went through and the fears soldiers and other people experienced. It is a way to say "thank you" for their bravery. The day reminds people of their responsibility to keep working for peace.

Canadian soldiers often serve as United Nations peacekeepers to help keep the world a peaceful place.

Two Minutes of Silence

On the 11th hour of the 11th day of the 11th month, people stop what they are doing and remember. This day and time was the official ending of World War I. People in schools, offices, and businesses stop their work and **bow** their heads.

November				S M T W T F

				S	M	T	W	T	F	
									1	
				3	4	5	6	7	8	
				10	11	12	13	14	15	
				17	18	19	20	21	22	
				24 31	25	26	27	28	29	

Wed	Thu	Fri	Sat
1	2		4
8	9	10	11
			Remembrance Day
15			18

Remembrance Day is marked on the calendar.

These people are bowing their heads on Remembrance Day.

For two whole minutes no one speaks. During these two minutes, people think about the soldiers, nurses, doctors, and other people who have served during times of war, conflict, and peace.

DID YOU KNOW?

During World War I, more than 600,000 Canadian soldiers volunteered to serve their country.

Poppies

Poppies are red flowers that people wear on Remembrance Day. People wear poppies because these flowers bloomed over the graves of dead soldiers in France and Belgium. Poppies bloomed on the battlefields called Flanders Fields.

● This poppy grows in a garden.

DID YOU KNOW?

*Many people thought poppies were **mysterious** flowers because they bloomed over the graves of dead soldiers.*

Poppies are a symbol of Remembrance Day. A symbol stands for or represents something else. Many people wear paper or plastic poppies during the week before Remembrance Day. They pin them on the left **lapel** of a jacket, close to the heart.

It is respectful to wear a poppy close to your heart.

11

Remembrance Day Poems

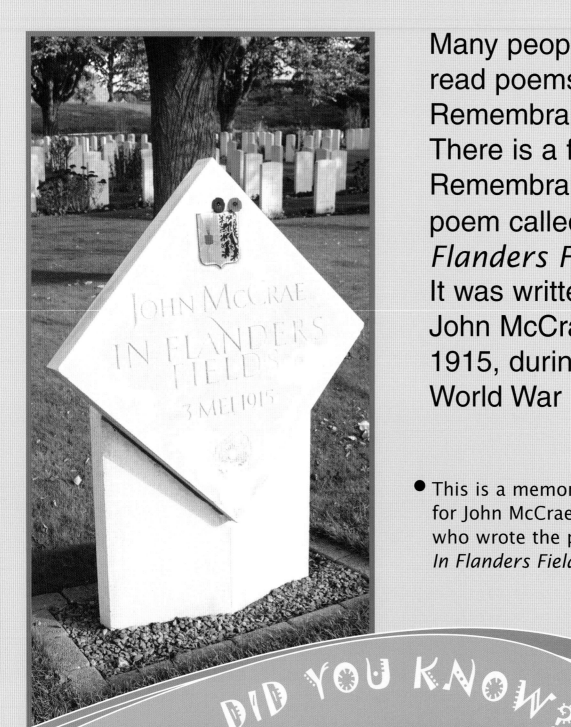

This is a memorial for John McCrae who wrote the poem *In Flanders Fields*.

Many people read poems on Remembrance Day. There is a famous Remembrance Day poem called *In Flanders Fields*. It was written by John McCrae in 1915, during World War I.

DID YOU KNOW?

John McCrae was a doctor and a teacher. He served in both the South African War and World War I.

These children are writing Remembrance Day poems.

Many Remembrance Day ceremonies include a reading of *In Flanders Fields*. There are other Remembrance Day poems, too. One poem begins like this:

"We wear a poppy on Remembrance Day, and at eleven we stand and pray..."

Parades

In some cities, there are Remembrance Day parades. **Veterans** march in the parades and wave to people as they walk by. Some people in the parades play drums or other instruments for others to listen to as they watch.

These people are at a Remembrance Day parade in Canada.

People carry or wave Canadian flags at Remembrance Day parades in Canada. People may also sing the Canadian national anthem. Remembrance Day is a day to feel patriotic, or proud of your country.

This girl is saying "thank you" to a Canadian veteran at a Remembrance Day parade.

DID YOU KNOW?

Attending a Remembrance Day parade or other ceremony is a great way to say "thank you" to people who serve their country.

National War Memorial

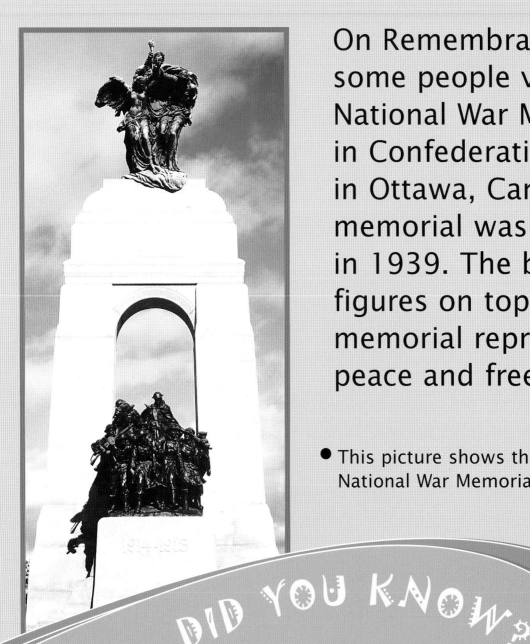

On Remembrance Day, some people visit the National War Memorial in Confederation Square in Ottawa, Canada. The memorial was **unveiled** in 1939. The bronze figures on top of the memorial represent peace and freedom.

• This picture shows the National War Memorial.

DID YOU KNOW?

In 1982, the bronze numbers, 1939–1945 and 1950–1953 (Korea), were added to honor the soldiers who lost their lives in World War II and the Korean War.

The memorial was designed to **commemorate** the 60,000 Canadians who died in World War I. Each bronze figure stands over 7.5 feet (2.2 meters) high. Each year, Remembrance Day ceremonies are held at the National War Memorial.

This picture gives a close look at a figure from the National War Memorial.

Tomb of the Unknown Soldier

The **Tomb** of the Unknown Soldier is a special tomb located next to the National War Memorial. It contains the remains of an unidentified World War I soldier.

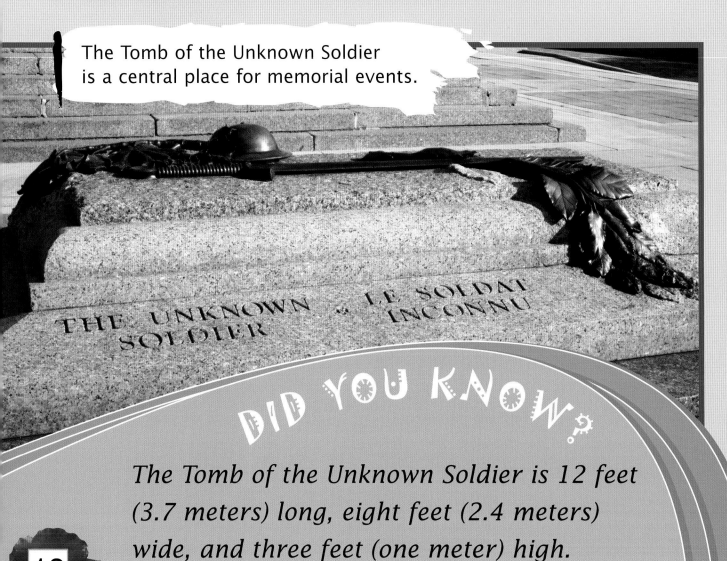

The Tomb of the Unknown Soldier is a central place for memorial events.

DID YOU KNOW?

The Tomb of the Unknown Soldier is 12 feet (3.7 meters) long, eight feet (2.4 meters) wide, and three feet (one meter) high.

The soldier's body was moved to Canada from a cemetery near Vimy Ridge in France. Many Canadians died there in a famous battle.

The tomb is a symbol. It represents all the Canadians in the Navy, Army, Air Force, or Merchant Marines who die serving their country. Many people place poppies on the tomb on Remembrance Day.

• It is important to pay respect to the soldiers on Remembrance Day.

Remembrance Day Wreaths

Wreaths are special, circular flower arrangements. On Remembrance Day, people lay wreaths at tombs or monuments as a way to honor those who have died.

This picture shows Remembrance Day wreaths.

DID YOU KNOW?

Some people attach special notes or poems to their Remembrance Day wreaths.

There are many different kinds of wreaths. You can make your own Remembrance Day wreath by pinning poppies to a circular band of green leaves. The red poppies will look especially bright against the green leaves. You can hang your wreath on a wall or a door.

• These children have made their own Remembrance Day wreath.

Candlelight Ceremonies

Remembrance Day candlelight ceremonies began in the Netherlands. People held the ceremonies to celebrate the Canadians who helped **liberate** them. Most candlelight ceremonies last for about 40 minutes.

These people are at a candlelight ceremony.

DID YOU KNOW?

*Everyone takes their candles with them at the end of a candlelight ceremony. The candles are **keepsakes** and remind people to share their experiences of the ceremony with family and friends.*

In 1995, Dutch children placed lit candles on the graves of Canadian soldiers. The candles stayed lit overnight and the bright glow drew people to the cemeteries.

• People light candles to show respect for those who died serving their country.

Posters

Each year, Veterans Affairs Canada comes out with a Remembrance Day poster. The poster is meant to remind Canadians of the sacrifices and achievements made by veterans during times of war and peace.

* This poster commemorates Veterans' Week in Canada.

November 11, 2009, marks the 91st anniversary of the end of World War I.

The Remembrance Day posters can include artwork and photographs. They mark special events or battles and try to show the personal sides of war. You can make a Remembrance Day poster, too!

These children are making Remembrance Day posters.

Around the World

Days of remembrance take place all over the world. In the United States, people celebrate Memorial Day on the last Monday in May. In the United Kingdom, Remembrance Sunday is on the second Sunday in November.

This picture shows a ceremony on Remembrance Sunday.

DID YOU KNOW?

People in France celebrate Armistice Day.

26

On Memorial Day, there are ceremonies at war memorials.

In Ireland, there is a National Day of Commemoration on the Sunday closest to July 11. All Irish men and women who died in wars are honored on this day. Jewish people observe **Holocaust** Remembrance Day at the end of April or at the beginning of May.

Spread the Word

Spread the word about Remembrance Day! Tell your family and friends about Remembrance Day events that you can attend together. Plan your own commemorative ceremony and invite the people in your neighborhood.

- Get others involved in Remembrance Day.

DID YOU KNOW?

Some people plant tulips or a tree in memory of people in their communities who have died during their military service.

On Remembrance Day, encourage your family and friends to say "thank you" to a veteran or Canadian Forces member. Ask the students at your school to write letters of thanks to give to veterans.

These children are saying, "thank you" to veterans.

Learn More!

Learn more about Remembrance Day, different Remembrance Day events and ceremonies, and why it is important to recognize this day. Share what you learn with your family and friends.

- Canada gives its veterans medals to honor their bravery and service. Learn more about them by asking a veteran.

DID YOU KNOW?

You can learn more about Remembrance Day by visiting the Kids' Zone at the Veterans Affairs Canada Web site at www.vac-acc.gc.ca.

This Canadian war memorial is in Afghanistan.

Research the Canadian memorial sites around the world. There are memorials built for Canadians in countries in Europe, Africa, and Asia. Memorials are usually placed at sites that were important during wartime.

Glossary

bow To bend the head

commemorate To call to memory or mark by a ceremony

Commonwealth An association of nations consisting of the United Kingdom, Canada, Australia, and several other countries

conflict A disagreement or struggle

Holocaust The killing of Jews by Nazis during World War II

honor To treat with respect

keepsake Something kept in memory of a person, place, or event

lapel The fold of the front of a coat that is usually part of the collar

liberate To set free

mysterious Describing something that cannot be explained

sacrifices Giving up things for the sake of someone else

tomb A chamber for a dead person

unveiled Revealed or uncovered

veterans Former members of the armed forces

Index